THE
DUNGEONS  DRAGONS®
COLORING BOOK

THE
DUNGEONS & DRAGONS®
COLORING BOOK

80 Adventurous Line Drawings

WIZARDS
OF THE COAST
OFFICIAL LICENSED PRODUCT

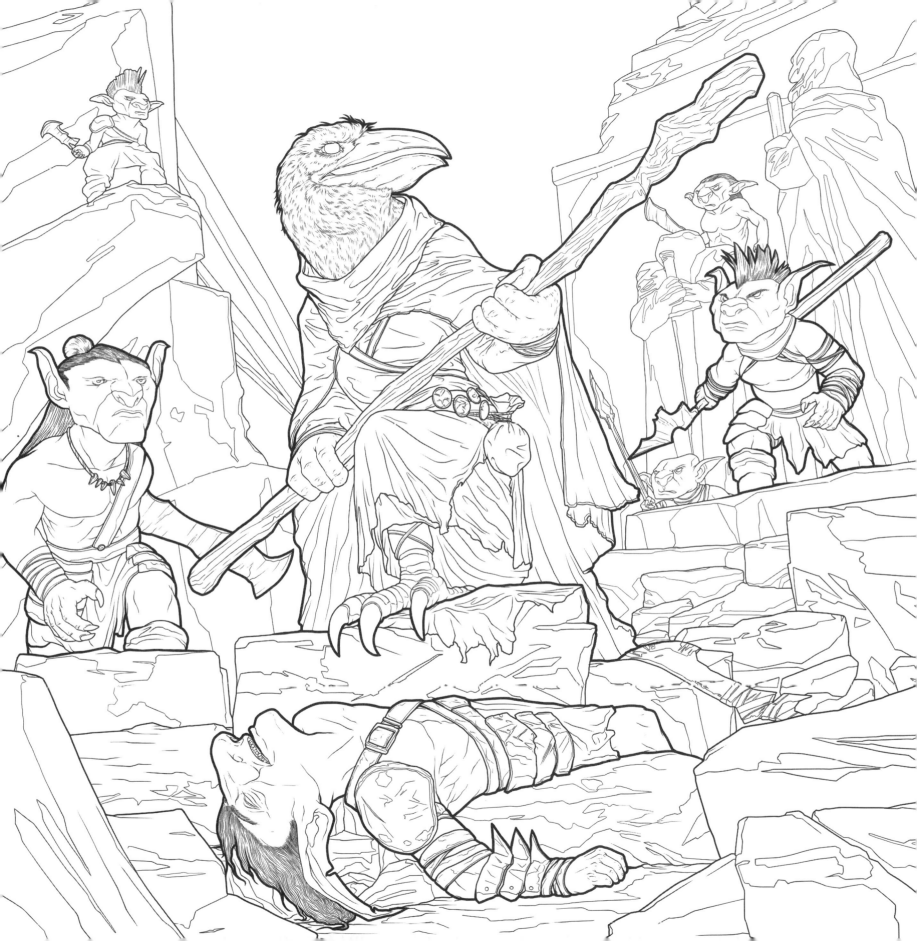

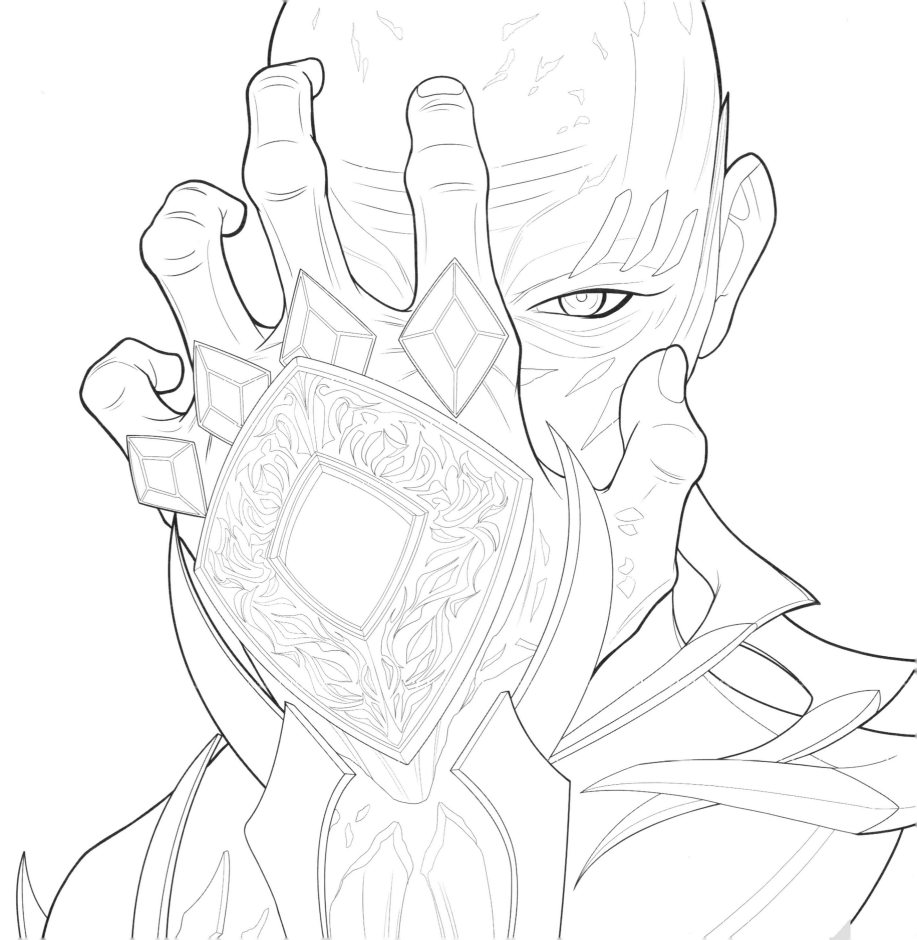

Wizards of the Coast, Dungeons & Dragons, D&D, their respective logos, Forgotten Realms,
and the dragon ampersand are registered trademarks of Wizards of the Coast LLC in the U.S.A. and
other countries. © 2023 Wizards of the Coast LLC. All rights reserved. Licensed by Hasbro.

All rights reserved.
Published in the United States by Ten Speed Press, an imprint of the
Crown Publishing Group, a division of Penguin Random House LLC, New York.
TenSpeed.com

Ten Speed Press and the Ten Speed Press colophon are
registered trademarks of Penguin Random House LLC.

Trade Paperback ISBN: 978-1-9848-6219-8

Printed in the USA

Acquiring editor: Shaida Boroumand | Project editor: Zoey Brandt | Production editor: Ashley Pierce
Designer: Isabelle Gioffredi | Art director: Betsy Stromberg
Illustrators: Cynthia Inesta, Andrea Santopietro, Gilangarmi Saputra, and Brandi York
Production manager: Dan Myers
Marketer: Paola Crespo

1st Printing

First Edition